Drawing Buddhas and Bodhisattvas

Faith Stone

SGRY 2013
Shoshoni Yoga Retreat
shoshoni.org

Published by SGRY
Prakasha Press
P.O. Box 206
Eldorado Springs, CO 80025
USA

Copyright © 2013 SGRY. All rights reserved

shoshoni.org
shambhava-bookstore.com

No part of this book may be reproduced or utilized by any means without prior written permission from the publisher SGRY.

ISBN 978-1-888386-18-9

Stone, Faith
Drawing Buddhas and Bodhisattvas
1st edition
Book design and layout by Kumara Etzel

1. Art-Technique 2. Yoga 3. Tibetan Studies 4. Drawing Buddhas
5. Stone, Faith
Drawing Buddhas and Bodhisattvas by Faith Stone

Printed in the United States

Contents

Introduction   *v*
How to Use This Book   *vi*
Dedication   *viii*

Part One: Buddhas

Buddha Head   3
Shakyamuni Buddha   5
Amitabha Buddha   11
Samantabhadra   13
Medicine Buddha   15

Part Two: Bodhisattvas and Peaceful Deities

Chenrezig   19
VajraSattva   21
PadmaSambhava   27
Manjusri   31
Green Tara   33
White Tara   39

Part Three: Semi Wrathful and Wrathful Deities

Achi Chokyi Drolma   43
VajraVarahi   47
VajraPani   51
VajraKilaya   55

Part Four: Guru Thangka

Rudi Thangka   59

To my husband
Baba Shambhavananda
whose devotion and encouragement
are my constant inspiration

Ganesha, the Remover of Obstacles

Introduction

As an artist and meditation practitioner, I studied Tibetan Thangka Painting at Naropa University in Boulder for 3 years under Sanje Elliot and also took a class with his colleague Cynthia Moku. Since then I have continued the practice of drawing Buddhas and Bodhisattvas under the guidance of the two brothers, the Venerable Khen Rinpoche and Khenpo Tsewang Dongyal, and also with the help and support of HH the Drikung Kagyu Chetsang Rinpoche. I've now been drawing and painting thangkas for 25 years.

In my studies and practice, I have found it difficult to find good thigse drawings of various Bodhisattvas and Buddhas. I began researching and then drawing thigse proportions with the idea of sharing them with other practitioners and those wishing to learn to draw Buddhas and Bodhisattvas. This is a thigse (proportions) drawing book, not a philosophical text. A qualified Buddhist teacher will greatly increase the richness of experience and understanding for the practitioner.

Always after drawing or painting sacred art, I do the dedication prayer taught to me by my teacher. I have included this dedication prayer in the book for you to use as well. This offers the merit or good karma for drawing Buddhas to all sentient beings. Buddhas and Bodhisattvas are sacred art and as such should not be treated too casually. You are creating an environment in which the Buddha will live. Drawings should be kept in a clean, safe place. If you want to dispose of a drawing or painting, it should be burned, not put in the trash.

Faith Stone

How to Use This Book

The ancient practice of drawing and painting Buddhas brings great richness into one's life. It is a very contemplative practice, increasing focus and directing one's attention in a very positive way. It's a creative meditation in action.

Thangka painting and drawing Buddhas is very different in nature from a Western approach to art. Expressing yourself is paramount in Western art but not so in the drawing of Buddhas, where you are trying to closely replicate the Buddha figure to the ideal proportions. Your goal is to try to stay out of the way and let the Buddha be expressed - not you. Essentially you are creating an environment for the Bodhisattva or Buddha to reside or take form. Traditionally students adhere closely to the thigse for the figure. It is in the landscape that you have the opportunity to express yourself.

The traditional way to draw a Buddha or Bodhisattva is with a thigse, a graph measurement. The measurements are called sor, which means finger and one sor equals the width of one finger. The exact measurement can be adjusted to the scale of the image – depending on how large or small you want the figure to be. I often use 4 sor to equal ½ inch. Once you have drawn the thigse or graph you are ready to draw the Buddha figure within these idealized proportions.

You start the process by first drawing the thigse and next the Buddha figure within the proportions. After drawing in pencil, ink the final figure in with a 10/0 brush and India ink. Then transfer the drawing to a larger paper in order to include the landscape and offerings. You can look at examples of these in the book. I would also recommend Tibetan Thangka Painting by David and Janice Jackson and Tibetan Buddhist Symbols by Robert Beer. These are both excellent references for furthering your understanding and practice of Tibetan art.

Please visit my website **faithstoneart.com** to see these drawings as completed paintings.

It is stated by the Tathagata:

"The essence of the whole teaching of the Buddha is represented in paintings. Those who know well how to paint will accumulate infinite merit. Those who look upon the paintings will have Buddhism opened up to them, and even very sinful people will come to believe in the Buddha when they see a single painted line, or just when they see the smallest corner of a painting. It is said by Gautama Buddha - whosoever beholds Buddhist pictures will be rewarded. Since those that merely look at a painting are blessed, how much greater will be the recompense of those with faith and devotion. And beyond conception will be the merits of those who paint the figure of the Buddha on cloth.

A glance at the image of the Buddha will bring benefits in number equal to the merits bestowed on those who serve the Buddhas, the Bodhisattvas, and the Arhats, and these are as numerous as the grains of sand in the Ganges."

From the translation of an inscription on a painting of Buddha –
Tibet, 18th century

Dedication Prayer

SÖ NAM DI YI TAM CHE ZIK PA NYI
By this virtue may we become enlightened, and

TOP NE NYE PAY DRA NAM PAM JE NE
having vanquished all negative influences,

KYE GA NA CHI BA LAP TRUK PA YI
liberate all beings from the ocean of existence,

SI PAY TSO LE DRO WA DROL WAR SHO
which is turbid with the waves of birth,
old age, sickness and death.

calligraphy by Sanje Elliot

Part One:
Buddhas

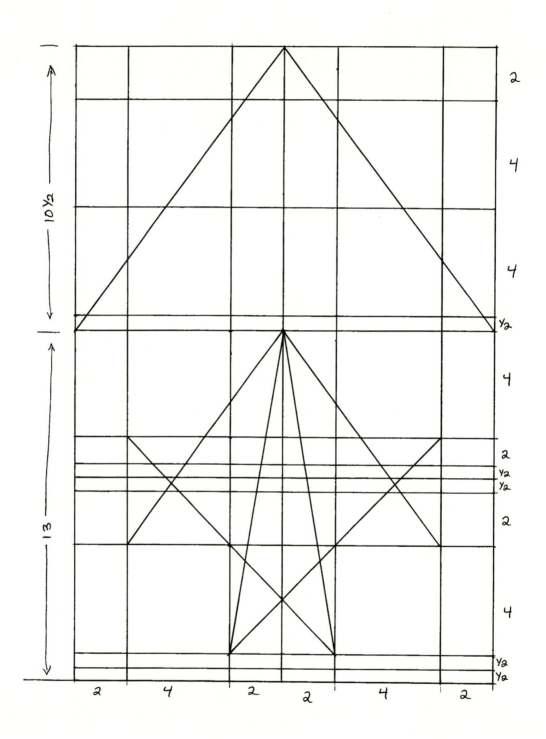

½ sor = 3/16 inch
1 sor = 3/8 inch
2 sor = 3/4 inch
4 sor = 1½ inch

Buddha head
thigse

Drawing Buddhas and Bodhisattvas

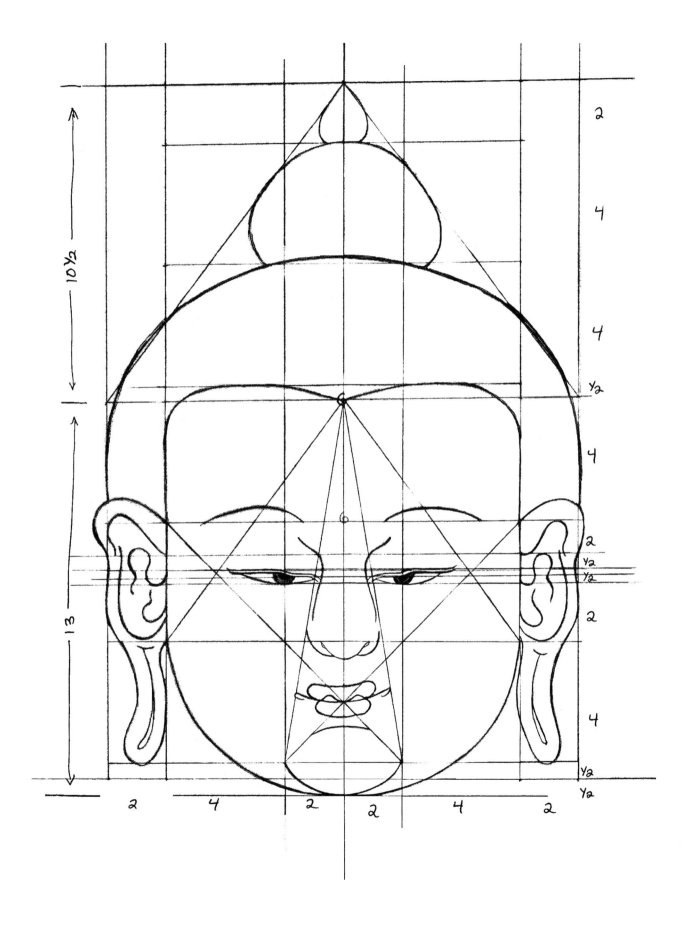

Buddha Head Thigse

Shakyamuni Buddha

ༀ་མུ་ནི་མུ་ནི་མ་ཧཱ་མུ་ནི་ཡེ་སྭཱ་ཧཱ།
oṃ muni muni mahā muniye svāhā

Shakyamuni Buddha is the historical Buddha. He is shown here with his right hand extending downward in the "Calling the earth to witness mudra". At the time of his enlightenment he is said to have touched his hand to the ground and called the earth to witness.

Shakyamuni wears Nirmanakaya robes - without adornment. These are the robes still worn by Tibetan Buddhist monks today. He holds a begging bowl.

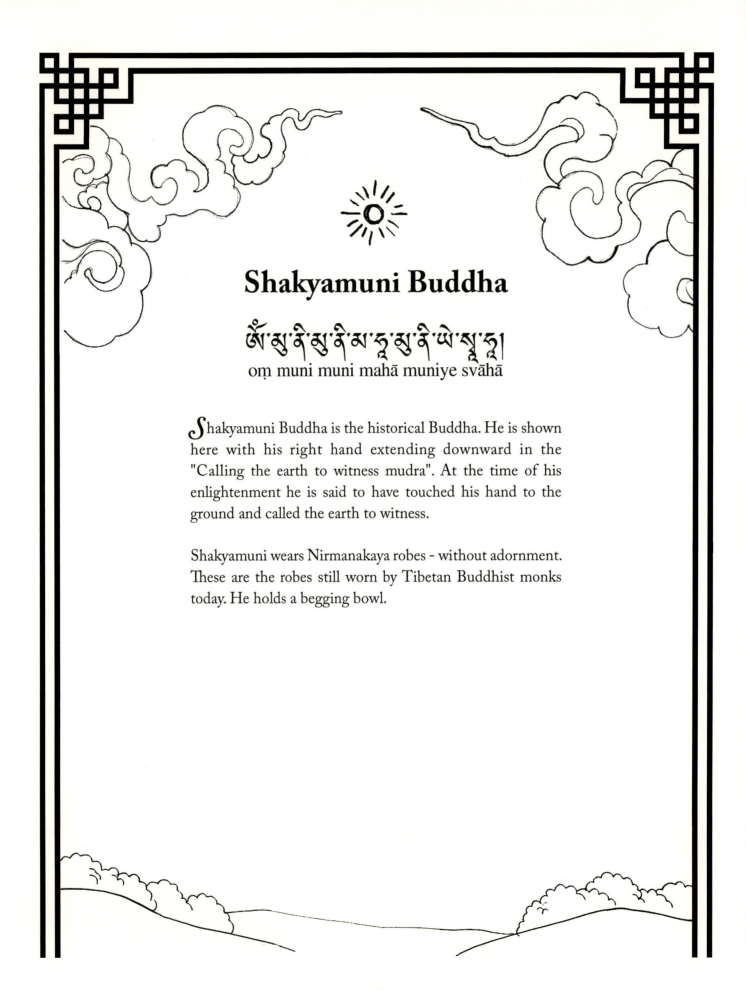

Shakyamuni Buddha

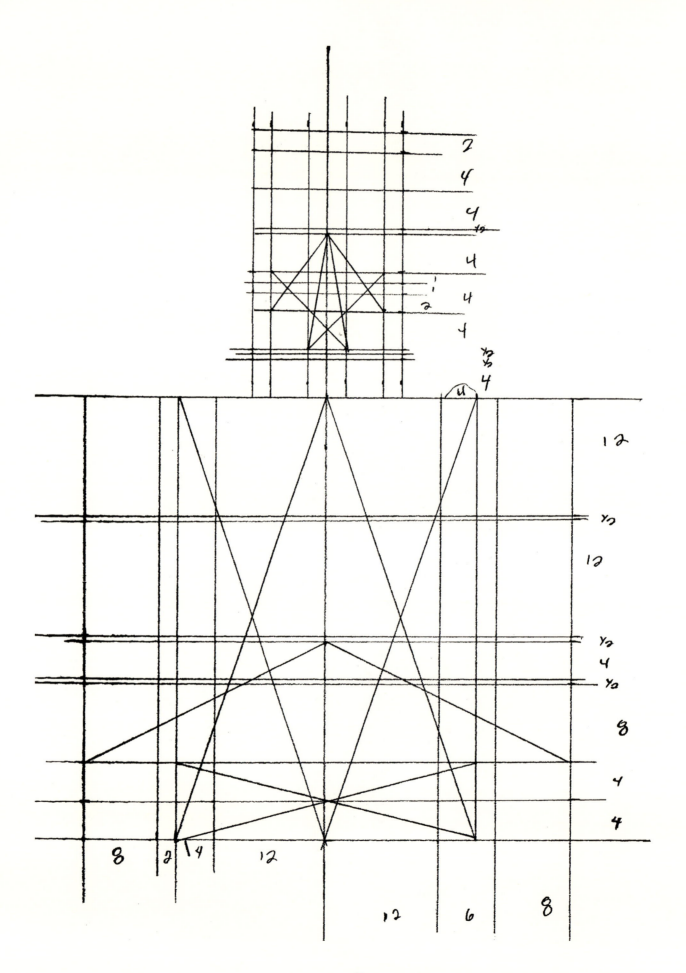

Shakyamuni Buddha Thigse

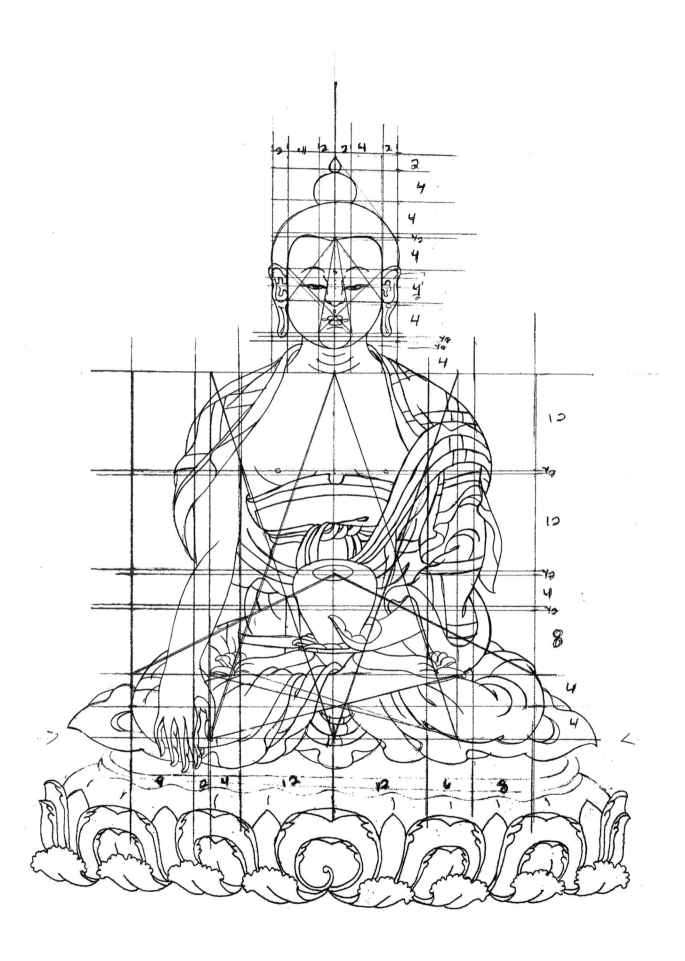

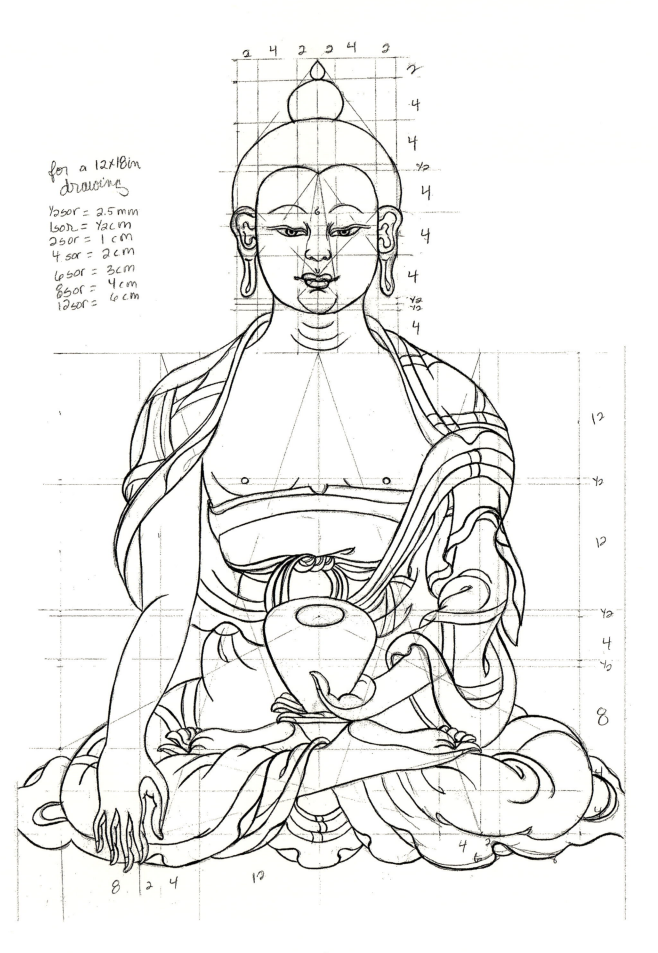

Shakyamuni Buddha

Shakyamuni Buddha

Amitabha

ༀ་ཨ་མི་དེ་ཝ་ཧྲཱིཿ
oṃ amideva hrīḥ

*A*mitabha translates as boundless light and boundless life. He is the Buddha in the Land of Ultimate Bliss (Pure Land) in which all beings enjoy unbounded peace and happiness. People recite his mantra and call upon his name at the time of dying to be reborn in Amitabha's Pure Land.

Drawing Buddhas and Bodhisattvas

Samantabhadra

ཨ་ཨོཾ་ཧཱུྃ།
ཨཱཿ་ཨ་དཀར་ས་ལེ་འོད་ཨ་ཡང་ཨོཾ་དུ།

a om hung
ah a kar sa le od a yang om du

Samantabhadra is the primordial Buddha and the embodiment of timeless awareness. He is the union of awareness and emptiness. The ultimate meaning of the Samantabhadra mantra is the essence of one's own mind. The particular benefit of the mantra is to remove obstacles from meditation and develop the clarity of "the view". It is known as the mantra of the Dharmakaya. It is the essence of the actual deity Samantabhadra, so as you recite it you become more closely identified with this deity and all of his perfected qualities. This is the purpose of mantra.

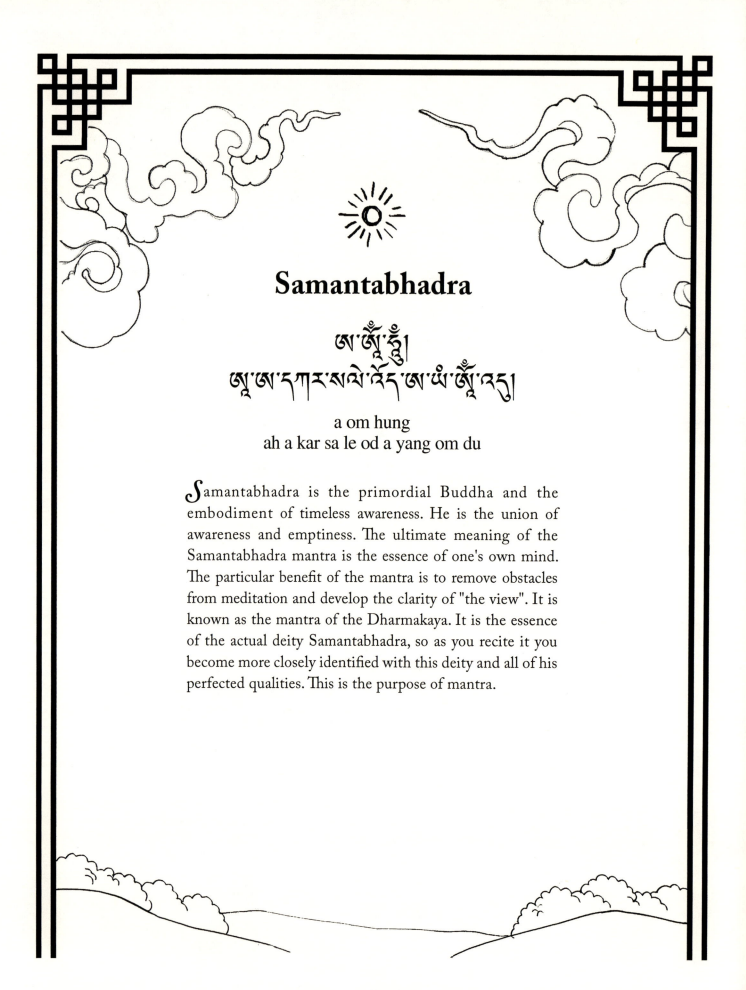

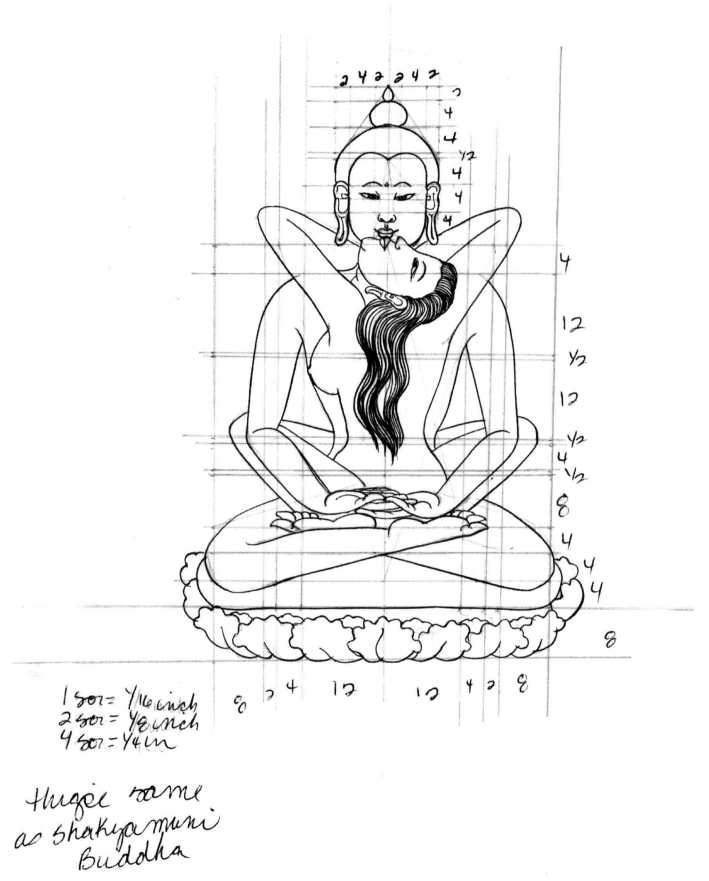

Medicine Buddha

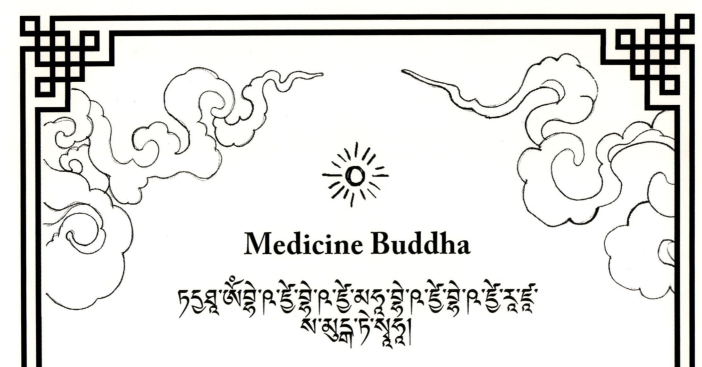

tadyathā oṃ bhekhaze bhekhaze mahā bhekhaze bhekhaze rāza samungate svāhā

Medicine Buddha is the healing Buddha. He is blue in color and holds a medicine plant in his right hand and a begging bowl with the medicine flower in his left hand. He is seated on a lion throne. He wears Nirmanakaya robes (without adornment) as still worn by Tibetan Buddhist monks today. Medicine Buddha practice cures physical, mental, and emotional illness.

Part Two:
Bodhisattvas and Peaceful Deities

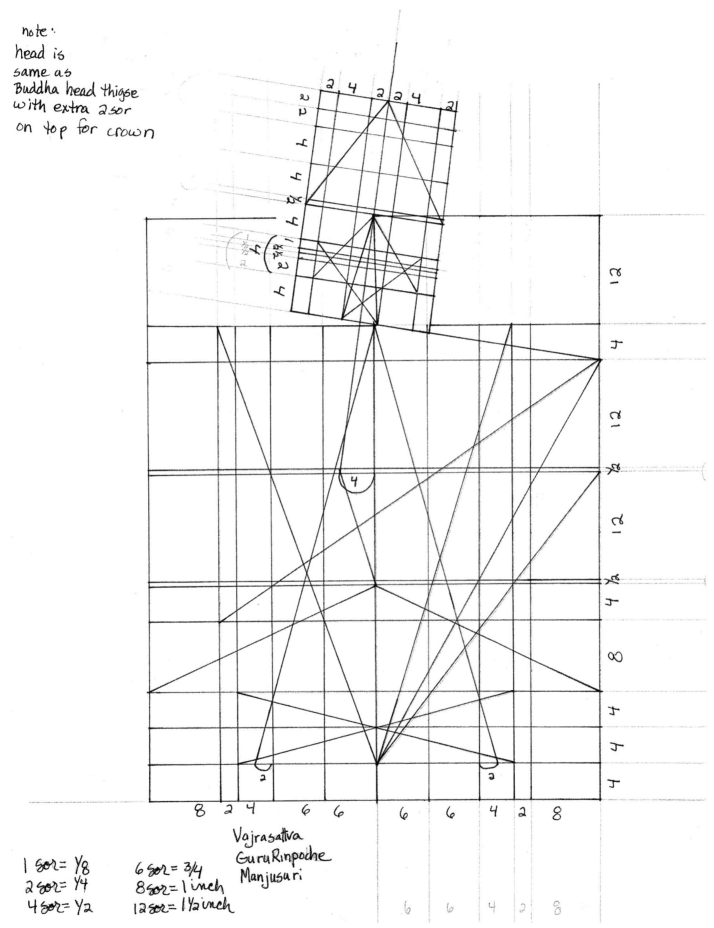

Chenrezig

ཨོཾ་མ་ཎི་པདྨེ་ཧཱུྃ།

oṃ maṇi padme hūṃ

*I*n the Tibetan Buddhist pantheon of enlightenend beings, Chenrezig is known as the embodiment of the compassion of all the Buddhas, the Bodhisattva of Compassion. Chenrezig, also known as Avalokiteshvara, is the earthly manifestation of the self-born, eternal Buddha, Amitabha. He guards this world in the interval between the historical Shakyamuni Buddha, and the Buddha of the future, Maitreya.

According to the dharma teachings, Chenrezig vowed that he would not rest until he had liberated all the beings in all the realms of suffering. This is referred to as the Bodhisattva vow. After working diligently at this task for a very long time, he looked out and realized the immense number of miserable beings yet to be saved. One version states that seeing this, he became despondent and his head split into thousands of pieces. Amitabha Buddha put the pieces back together as a body with very many arms and many heads, so that Chenrezig could work with countless beings all at the same time. He is often depicted with eleven heads, and a thousand arms fanned out around him.

Chenrezig may be the most popular of all Buddhist deities, except for Buddha himself. He is beloved throughout the Buddhist world. He is known by different names in different lands: as Avalokiteshvara in the ancient Sanskrit language of India, as Kuan-yin in China, and as Kannon in Japan.

Drawing Buddhas and Bodhisattvas

20 Chenrezig

VajraSattva

ཨོཾ་བཛྲ་སཏྭ་ས་མ་ཡ་མ་ནུ་པཱ་ལ་ཡ། བཛྲ་སཏྭ་ཏྭེ་ནོ་པ་ཏིཥྛ་
དྲྀ་ཌྷོ་མེ་བྷ་བ། སུ་ཏོ་ཥྱོ་མེ་བྷ་བ། སུ་པོ་ཥྱོ་མེ་བྷ་བ།
ཨ་ནུ་རཀྟོ་མེ་བྷ་བ། སརྦ་སིདྡྷི་མྨེ་པྲ་ཡཙྪ། སརྦ་ཀརྨ་སུ་ཙ་མེ
ཙིཏྟཾ་ཤྲི་ཡཿ་ཀུ་རུ་ཧཱུྃ། ཧ་ཧ་ཧ་ཧ་ཧོཿ བྷ་ག་བཱན་ སརྦ་
ཏ་ཐཱ་ག་ཏ་བཛྲ་མཱ་མེ་མུཉྩ། བཛྲཱི་བྷ་བ་མ་ཧཱ་ས་མ་ཡ་ སཏྭ་ ཨཱཿ ༎
ཧཱུྃ་ ཕཊ྄་

    oṃ vajra-sattva sa-maya, manu pa-laya
    vajra-sattva tenopa tish-ta dado-me bhava
    suto-khyo-me bhava, supo-khyo-me bhava
    anu-rakto-me bhava, sarva siddho-me pra-yat-sha
    sarva karma su-tse-me, tsi-tan, shri-ya kuru hung
    ha-ha ha-ha-ho bhag-a-wan
    sarva ta-tha-ga-tha vajra ma-me mun-tsa
    vajri-bha-wa maha-samaya sa-to-ah

    Short mantra: om vajrasattva hung

VajraSattva practice is a tantric meditation done for the purification of karma. As a Mahayana practice, it is undertaken with a bodhichitta aim to purify all our karma in order to reach enlightenment as quickly as possible. Then we are best able to help all sentient beings. On an ultimate level, VajraSattva practice is nonconceptual meditation on emptiness.

VajraSattva mantra is the 100-syllable mantra and is one of the nondro, preliminary, practices in Tibetan Buddhism. VajraSattva is white in color and holds a vajra/dorje and a bell. He wears the crown and jewels of Sambhogakaya.

VajraSattva

VajraSattva

VajraSattva with landscape and offerings

PadmaSambhava

oṃ āḥ hūṃ vajra guru padma siddhi hūṃ

𝓟admaSambhava, the Lotus Born, is the Yogi from India who brought Buddhism to Tibet. He is also known as Guru Rinpoche or Precious Guru. He holds a vajra/dorje in his right hand and a begging bowl filled with nectar in his left hand. He has a staff with three heads on his left.

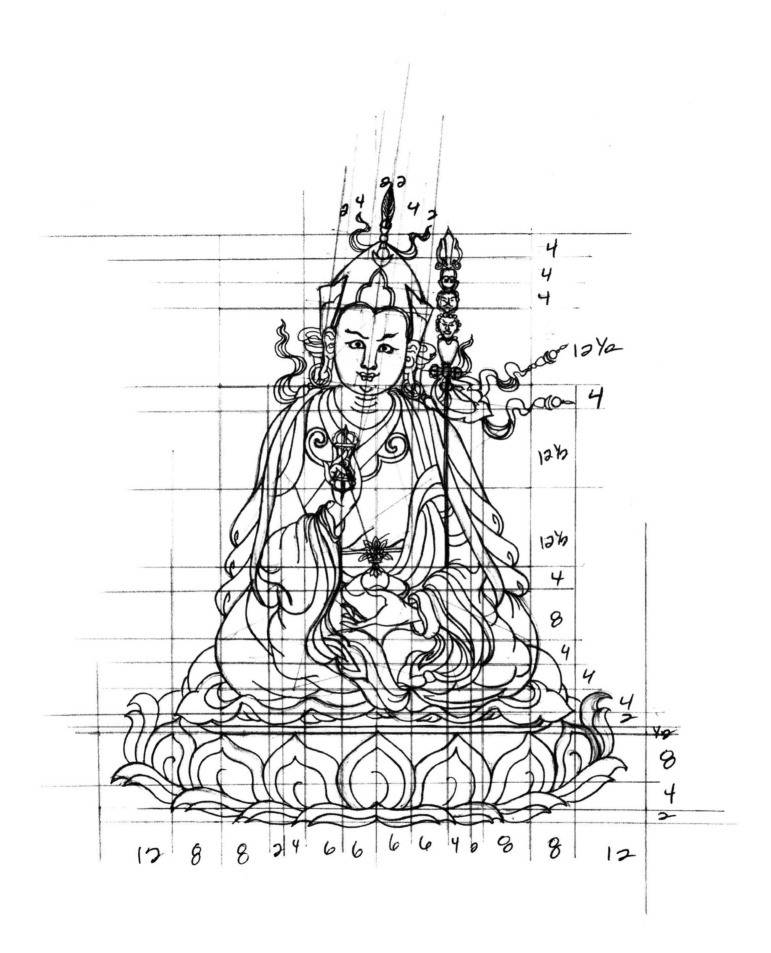

PadmaSambhava

PadmaSambhava

Manjusri

oṃ a ra pa tsa na dhīḥ

Manjusri is the Bodhisattva of wisdom and knowledge. He is red in color although all Buddhas can be gold in color. He holds a sword to cut through ignorance in his right hand and the Book of Knowledge in his left.

Manjusri

Green Tara

oṃ tāre tuttāre ture svāhā

*G*reen Tara is the Buddha in feminine form. She is considered the most accessible Goddess. Her right leg comes down off her lotus as an expression of, "Here I come to help." She is the embodiment of wisdom and compassion.

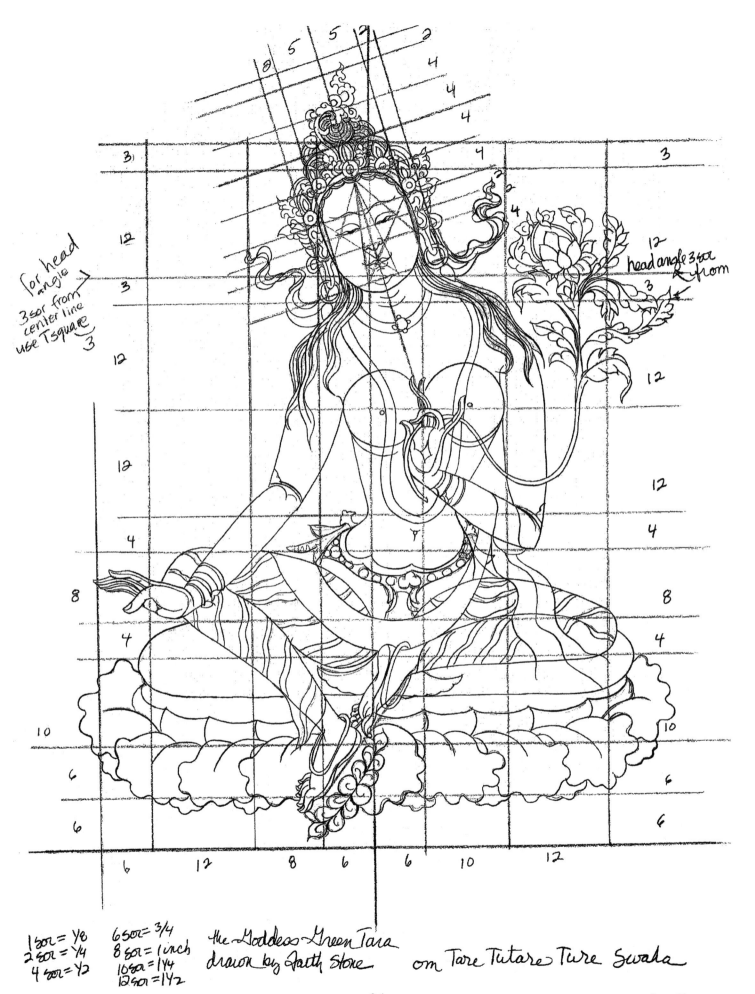

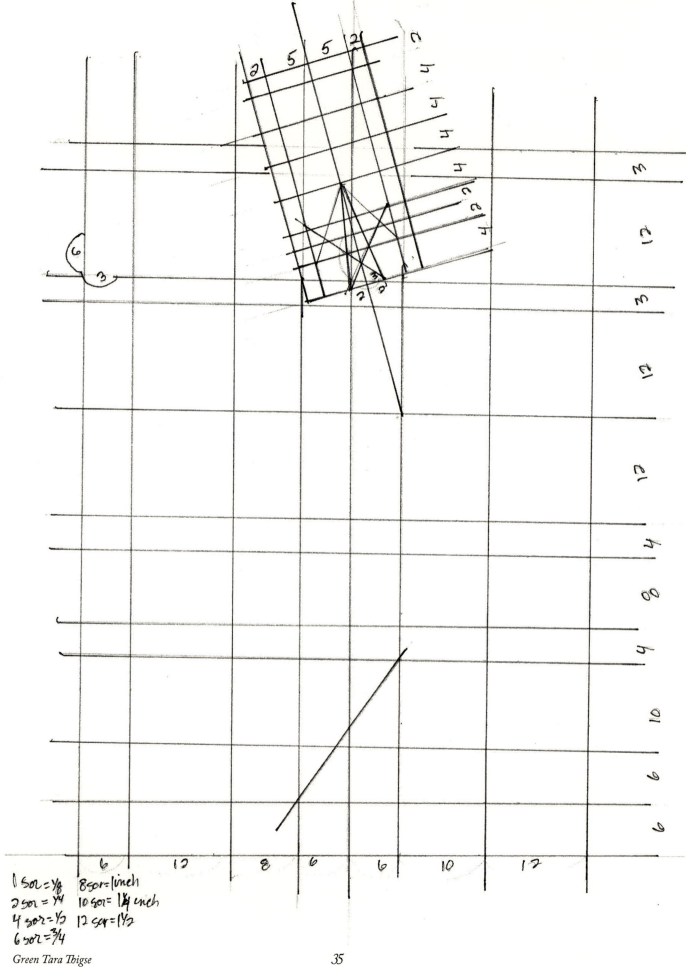

Green Tara Thigse

Green Tara head detail

Green Tara with landscape and offerings

White Tara

oṃ tāre tuttāre ture svāhā

White Tara is the embodiment of wisdom and compassion. She is the Buddha in feminine form. White Tara has seven eyes: two on her feet, two on her palms, and two on her face plus her third eye in the center of her forehead. This represents her ability to see and be aware of those in need. White Tara is associated with long life. She wears the crown and adornments of Sambhogakaya.

Part Three:
Semi Wrathful and Wrathful Deities

Achi Chokyi Drolma

oṃ mama tsakra soha
yar du sarwa du
ra dza ra dza du
mama du
hung phat soha

Short mantra: om mama tsakra soha

Mother Achi was the great grandmother to Lord Jigten Sumgon, founder of the Drikung Lineage. To this day she remains a great dharma protector of the Buddha's teachings. She is the emanation of VajraYogini who is the embodiment of the wisdom and compassion of all the Buddhas. She is the divine mother of the Buddhas and manifested out of compassion in the form of the Dakinis of the Five Buddha Families.

As a protectress Achi is visualized on her blue wisdom horse to symbolize the swiftness of her enlightened activities. She holds a wish-fulfilling jewel to symbolize her ability to bestow everything needed and desired when asked.

Achi Chokyi Drolma

Achi Chokyi Drolma with landscape and offerings

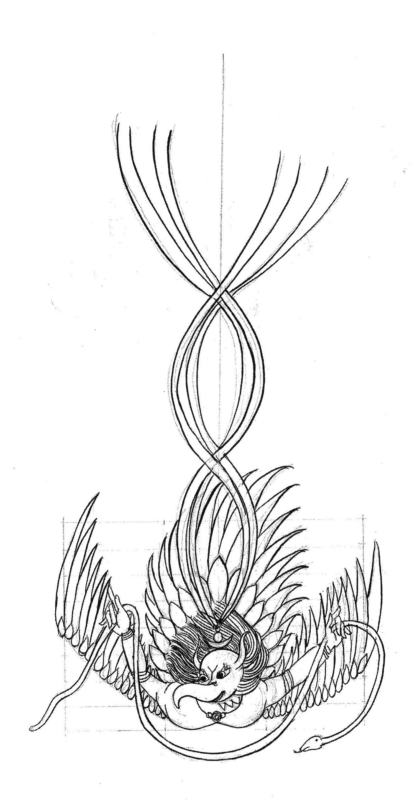

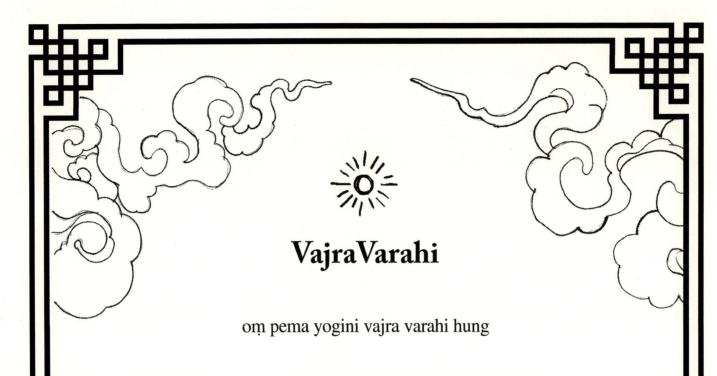

VajraVarahi

oṃ pema yogini vajra varahi hung

𝒱ajraVarahi is a form of VajraYogini, the diamond female yogini. She is the highest Yoga Tantra and as such she is considered to be a female Buddha. In her form as VajraVarahi, she has a sow's head in her hair. She holds a flayer in her right hand and scull cup filled with blood in her left hand. She has a staff with three heads.

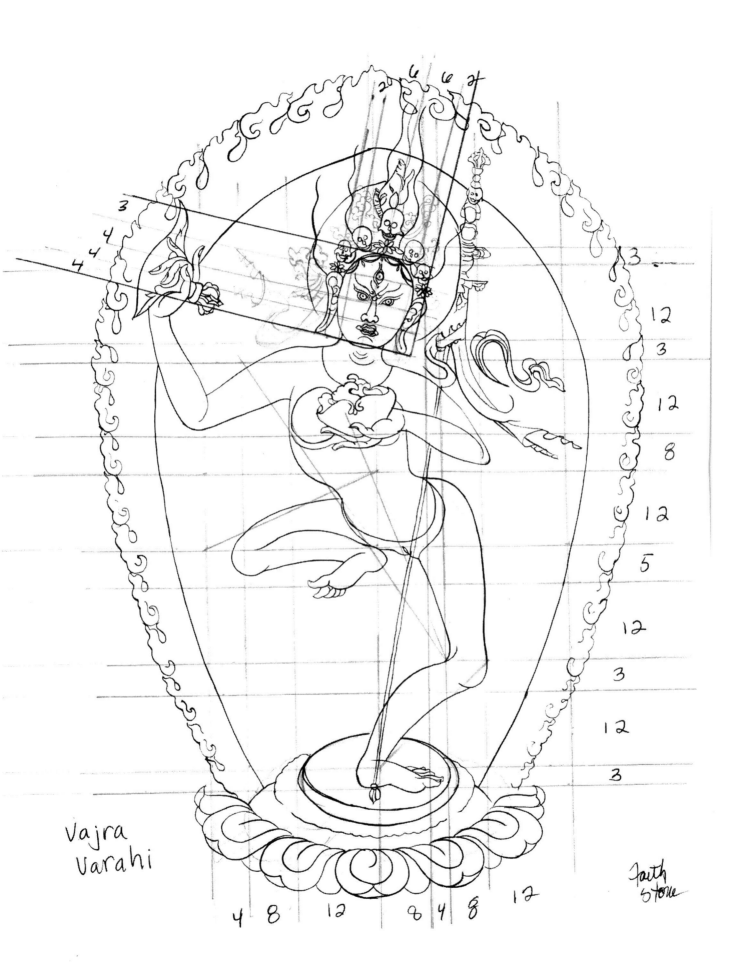

Vajra Varahi

VajraVarahi with landscape and offerings

VajraPani

ༀ་བཛྲ་པཱ་ཎི་ཧཱུྂ།
oṃ vajrapāṇi hūṃ

𝒱ajraPani (Holder of the Thunderbolt) represents the energy of the enlightened mind, and energy that breaks through delusion. He is a protector deity and is said to devour ghosts. VajraPani is pictured dancing wildly within a halo of flames, which represent transformation. He holds a hook in his left hand, and a vajra (thunderbolt) in his right hand to cut through the darkness of delusion.

VajraPani

VajraPani head detail

VajraKilaya

ཨོཾ་བཛྲ་ཀཱི་ལི་ཀཱི་ལ་ཡ་སརྦ་བིགྷནན་ཏྲིག་ནན་བཾ་ཧཱུྃ་ཕཊ྄༔

oṃ vajra ki li ka la ya sarva bighanan trig nan bam hung phat
oṃ vajra kili kalaya sarva bighnen trignen bam hung phet

*V*ajraKilaya is a significant Vajrayana deity who transmutes and transcends obstacles and obscurations. He is also understood as the embodiment of Buddha mind. He is a wrathful deity. This particular VajraKilaya is two armed and special to the venerable Khen Rinpoche and Khenpo Tsewanfg Dongyal. This drawing and painting were done under their guidance. Thangka painters traditionally study and copy the drawings of master painters. Students of the Khenpos took photos of this painting to Nepal where the local Thagnka painters copied my drawing and painting. I was so fortunate to have my painting multiply in this way.

VajraKilaya with landscape and offerings

Part Four:
Guru Thangka

Rudi Thangka

*T*his is a thangka painting in the Guru thangka or lineage thangka tradition. The central figure is Rudi (Swami Rudrananda), my first Guru. The setting is Eldorado Canyon where I live. Rudi is attended by Babaji Shambhavananda, one of his primary students. PadmaSambhava is in the sky overhead and the protector deity, VajraPani in the bottom left. The water buffaloes represent Rudi's idea of grinding up tensions like a water buffalo hitched to a grinding stone. There are a pair of local magpies in the tree.

Rudi Thangka

also available from
SHOSHONI YOGA RETREAT

The Shoshoni Cookbook
Anne Saks and Faith Stone

Yoga Kitchen
Faith Stone and Rachael Guidry

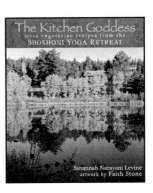

The Kitchen Goddess
Susannah Narayani Levine
artwork by Faith Stone

Rudi and the Green Apple
Faith Stone

Spontaneous Recognition
Sri Shambhavananda

A Seat by the Fire
Sri Shambhavananda

Purchase these titles from your local bookstore or directly from:

Shoshoni Yoga Retreat
P.O. Box 400
Rollinsville, CO 80474
(303) 642-0116

also available online at:
shoshoni.org

Sacred Journey
Swami Kripananda